inbound MARKETING

Why Certain Companies Profit More from Their Marketing than Others

By Brodie G. Tyler

INBOUND MARKETING: Why Certain Companies Profit More from Their Marketing than Others

Copyright © 2014 Brodie G. Tyler. All rights reserved.

No part of this book may be reproduced in any form or by any electronic or mechanical means including information storage and retrieval systems without permission in writing from the publisher or author except by a reviewer who may quote brief passages.

ISBN: 978-1502599223

Printed in the United States of America
First Edition

www.brodietyler.com

To my wife, Lindsey. When we met, I was homeless and living out of the back of my retail store just to get the business off the ground. Thanks for seeing past that and for supporting me as an entrepreneur all these years.

While the stories and examples that follow are real,
the names are fictitious to protect the privacy
of the individuals and companies.

Contents

FOREWORD By Dave Dee	9
PREFACE	13
1 • More Power In Your Hands	19
2 • 7 Ways Inbound Marketing Pays	29
3 • Has Your Marketing Changed With The Times?	37
4 • Inbound vs. Outbound Marketing	43
5 • The Inbound Marketing Triangle	51
6 • Why Your Content Should Be CRAP	55
7 • A Surprising Approach to Optimization	65
8 • Getting Published The Easy Way	71
9 • Have a Website You Can Be Proud Of	75
10 • How to Ethically Manipulate Google	81
11 • Blogging Your Way to Profits	89
12 • What You May Not Know About Email Marketing	101
13 • Reputation Equals Revenue	105
14 • Finally Making Social Media Successful	113
15 • Secrets to Winning Your Online Election	121
AFTERWORD	129

Foreword
By: Dave Dee

Finding Your Inner-Entertainer

Dan Kennedy and I were having lunch together one day when he was telling me a story. He was in an office supply store looking for a copy of "Success Magazine" which he was being featured in. The problem was, he couldn't find the magazine. All he found were tabloid and entertainment magazines.

So, he asked the manager, "How come you don't have Success Magazine in here?"

"Well," the manager replied, "because no one is

reading that stuff anymore. We may sell three copies a month of that magazine while all these others – all these entertainment-based magazines are flying off the shelves."

Remember, this was a store that sold office supplies to businesses and entrepreneurs!

People love to hear stories, even in the business world. They want to be entertained. It's why the teachers who educate our children get paid next to nothing compared to the movie stars who entertain them.

I too was an entertainer, performing a magic and mind reading show on stage for many years at corporate events, award dinners, and things like that. In the process I came to discover the secrets of truly capturing the attention of an audience.

Today, you still will find me on stage, but instead of reading people's minds, I'm likely revealing those sales and marketing secrets to a large audience of entrepreneurs and business owners.

All this brings me back to the reason why you're holding this book in your hands.

You have something to sell, and you'd like to sell more of it. Am I right?

Whatever business you're in, you're no different than I am (except for the stage). Just like me, you have a story to share with your audience. Obviously, that story needs to resonate with them and be entertaining if you want to sell anything. And finally, you need to communicate using the right tools so your audience will consume your story and take action.

This is inbound marketing at its core. And naturally, the book you're holding will walk you though the very process of crafting your message and sharing it in an optimized manner. Not to trick Google, but to really connect with your audience and improve your online visibility.

There's a reason why I've made nearly 500 posts to my blog at www.davedee.com.

There's a reason why I regularly engage in email marketing with my list of customers and prospects.

There's a reason why I'm active on social media platforms like Facebook and Twitter.

All this is inbound marketing. The reason I do it is because it helps me connect with my audience and add digits to my bank account balance.

Successful business people understand the value of creating entertaining content and regularly publishing it for their audience. Fortunately for you, Brodie Tyler happens to be the expert when it comes to this stuff.

In fact, I've known Brodie for years now and have personally hired him and his team for some of my own inbound marketing needs.

My word of advice is not to just read this book, but consume it. Apply it to your business and get on the inbound marketing path to success. You and your bank account will be glad you did!

Kick butt, make mucho "DEEnero!"

Dave Dee
The Psychic Salesman
www.davedee.com

Preface

A small dental practice experienced the enormous power of inbound marketing after only a couple of months of implementing it. One of the things we're doing for them at my company, Inbound Systems, is managing their content marketing, including their blog and social media.

Just today, we received a random call from the in-house person who manages their marketing. She relayed the story of how one of the blog posts we wrote for them attracted a patient from 250 miles away.

Now why would a patient drive past countless other dental offices to be treated at our customer's practice? It turns out that a simple blog post we wrote for the practice about a particular dental technology addressed the patient's needs perfectly. In this case, the practice was positioned as the expert on this technology in their field and left little choice for the patient who wanted that particular treatment.

A simple blog post like this is just a tip of the iceberg! Whether you market a small dental practice or a large Fortune 500 company, inbound marketing is quickly becoming mandatory if you want to compete in the business world of the 21st century.

You're One Of The Smart Ones

I purposefully wrote this book in a simple, dumbed-down manner. By all means, I'm not calling you dumb! The fact that you're reading this book proves quite the opposite.

I just don't want the vitally important message about inbound marketing to get lost in the details. I don't want you to get overwhelmed because the reality is, implementing inbound marketing can seem like a daunting task. I'm trying to combat that and will make it as easy as possible to understand and take action on.

Plus, even if you implement just 20% of what is revealed in the rest of this book, you're going to be 100% ahead of your competitors. So, I don't see a need to muddy the waters with unnecessary crap.

Get Comfy, You're In For A Ride

Hopefully you are reading this book in search of clarity when it comes to marketing in today's online, fast-paced, social climate. As you'll soon come to discover, this book is full of tips and tricks to getting the most out of inbound marketing for your business. It's just the beginning of a fun, new ride taking your company to the next level.

However, what you do with what you're about to learn is up to you.

Will it be easy?

Nope.

Will it double your sales by next month?

Unlikely.

Will it be worth your while?

Absolutely.

To your inbound marketing success,

Brodie Tyler
www.brodietyler.com
www.inboundsystems.com

What's the value of information if you don't do anything with it, right?

Knowledge is worth nothing without action!

So if you haven't already done so, make it easier to implement all the inbound marketing strategies you're about to learn. Visit the website below for my Inbound Marketing Checklist, free of charge:

www.brodietyler.com/inboundchecklist

Chapter 1

More Power In Your Hands

I couldn't tell you the exact year it was, but I was probably a young brace-face teenager the first time the internet made an impact on my life.

It was in the suburbs of Phoenix, Arizona where my family lived in a modest split level house. We kept our computer desk downstairs and my little brother, Chance, seemed to always be messing around on it.

Remember that whiney, cranky sound our 56k modems used to make? You couldn't be on the phone and the internet at the same time. Boy, was it rough in those days!

Anyway, I didn't fully grasp what the modem did or what exactly the internet was. I was still happy that my parents supplied us with a set of World Book

Encyclopedias (printed and bound as books!) and our first-generation Nintendo game console. Why did I need the internet when I had Super Mario?

After school one afternoon, Chance called me downstairs to look at what he was doing on the computer. I peered over his shoulder and he was typing away at the keyboard. He would stop typing, and then a few seconds later, more text would appear on the screen.

"Cool, how did you do that?" I asked.

"I'm chatting with somebody," he answered. "It's called a chat room."

The puzzled look on my face made it clear that I had no clue what he was talking about. He explained that there was somebody on the other end of the internet with whom he was chatting with, kind of like a telephone but with just text.

"Haha, no way," I responded. "There's no way that's possible." I walked away in utter disbelief and positive that my brother had gone crazy... either that or he was just messing around with me.

Looking back and seeing how far technology and the internet have come, I can only laugh at myself... especially since I am now the author of this book that has so much to do with the internet!

Technology moves and evolves at such a fast pace, doesn't it? And it's not slowing down either.

MORE POWER IN YOUR HANDS

The internet is here to stay, and as an entrepreneur, it is virtually impossible to ignore it as a means for marketing your business.

Let me ask, when was the last time you used a phone book to look up a business? If I could bet on it, I would guess quite a long time.

Just recently I was speaking in front of hundreds of business owners and entrepreneurs at a marketing conference. To illustrate a point, I asked them to raise their hands if they used a printed phone book on a regular basis. Not to my surprise, just two lonely souls raised their hand.

Why? Because we have access to information quicker than ever thanks to our computers, smartphones and tablets. We know what it means when somebody says to "google it." We're in the thick of the information age.

As far as your business is concerned, the internet is where your audience is. They're searching for what you sell on search engines like Google, Bing and Yahoo. They are telling their friends on Facebook and Twitter that they just made a purchase at your place of business. They're visiting sites like Yelp and Citysearch to read reviews of other businesses in your local area.

The internet is where your audience is. So, the internet is where your business needs to be visible.

Change Is Here

My goal here is quite simple. I simply want to change the way you view marketing your business on the internet.

Why? Because things are rapidly evolving, and once you grasp the concepts behind inbound marketing, and update your approach to marketing online...

...you'll worry less about Google's changes...

...you'll experience better visibility...

...you'll drive more traffic to your website...

...you'll delight your prospects and customers...

...and ultimately, you'll make more money.

Isn't that why you invest in marketing in the first place? To increase revenue and make money? Whatever your end goal is, inbound marketing (and more money for that matter) can help you get there.

The True Value of Inbound Marketing

Every business needs customers in order to thrive and survive. Yours is no different, so let me ask you a few important questions...

- **What would it mean to you if you didn't have to worry month in and month out how you're going to replace those customers who are done buying from you?** Every customer has a shelf life and is bound to stop buying from you sooner or later.

- **What would growing the number of new customers, patients or clients you get from the internet by 10%, 50%, or even 100% mean for your business?** Depending on your industry, you could upgrade equipment, redesign your building, parlay the revenue into other marketing to grow exponentially faster, take on more employees, buy out a competing business, and so on.

- **What would this type of growth mean for you personally?** You could qualify for a raise or promotion. You might sock away funds for retirement at a more rapid pace. You may want to upgrade your house, have more freedom to spend time with your family the way you want, and travel the way you've always dreamed.

Who Inbound Marketing Is For

Frankly, it's difficult for me to imagine a single business that cannot benefit from the principles of inbound marketing.

Whether you're a marketing manager or business owner, if you would like your company to grow at a more rapid pace, then you'll find inbound marketing especially appealing.

Or, perhaps you prefer to just grow slowly and

build a more predictable avenue of generating new clients, customers, patients or referral partners.

You'll even find the ideas I'm going to share with you useful if you simply want to retain the customer base you currently have. You and I both know that you have competitors who would love to just steal them!

Finally, inbound marketing is for you if you would like to maintain a 5 star reputation online. Whether you like it or not, others are going to talk about you and your company on the internet. It might as well be positive, right?

Square Peg In A Round Hole?

However, inbound marketing is NOT for you if you are seeking for a get-rich-quick type of marketing. Yes, some of our customers at Inbound Systems have experienced a windfall of new revenue almost immediately after implementing their inbound marketing efforts. Typically though, this is the exception rather than the rule.

Think of inbound marketing as a freight train. It takes a lot of energy to get moving. However, once it's going, there's no stopping the machine.

If you do it right, inbound marketing can produce predictable results for you long after you take your foot off the gas. (More on this later.)

What You Will Learn

I'm going to be an open book and show you how we help our customers get new customers, clients and patients from the internet, or more specifically, from inbound marketing strategies.

You're going to discover the same strategies we've used, as an example, to take one of our customers from a few thousand dollars of annual revenue generated from inbound marketing to approximately $260,000 just two years later.

You're going to see how implementing just one simple strategy resulted in $41,500 worth of sales for another customer.

You're going to understand how to build a virtual fence around your audience so they don't get poached by your competitors.

At the same time, you're going to learn important methods to protecting your reputation on the internet and maintaining a 5 star reputation, even on "mafia" style websites like Yelp. (If you've felt like you've been held hostage by Yelp, you know what I mean.)

An Entrepreneur's Heart Palpitations

I remember when we were struggling as a new business. As the sole breadwinner for my family, the weight of responsibility was completely on my shoulders. My anxiety levels were so high that many nights

I would just lay in bed wide awake, staring at the ceiling, wondering how I was going to pay the bills. I recall placing my hand over my chest and feeling my heart pound with nervousness. Even as I recount this agonizing experience, my heart rate is increasing because of how real that fear was.

Have you been there too?

Thankfully, I avoided utter catastrophe and was able to pull out of that funk. I'll tell you what though... They say that money can't buy you happiness, but I know it can sure buy you sleep!

This is the very reason why I love marketing and believe in it wholeheartedly. And as you'll read shortly, inbound marketing is a big part of that belief.

Marketing Math

Obviously, the more you can invest in profitable marketing, the better. I'm going to reveal why this is.

Personally, I was never a big fan of school. I did, however, always have a knack for math. So, let's do a little exercise to explain how to best leverage your marketing dollars.

Imagine I'm holding a $2.00 bill.

Would you buy it from me for $1.00?

Unless your name is Uncle Sam, of course you would!

Would you buy a $100 bill from me for $50?

It goes without saying, right? As elementary as this exercise is, this is how you have to look at the money you're spending on marketing, including the inbound marketing strategies I'm going to share with you in this book. There are two principles I abide by when it comes to marketing as a whole:

Principle #1: Any dollar I spend on marketing must produce more in return.

Principle #2: When marketing has proven to be profitable, spend as much as possible on it.

For illustration, let's imagine you sell business machines (or if you're in a different industry, insert your own numbers here). If an average customer brings in $70,000 of revenue, let's say after your hard costs there is $6,000 left over. Should you be willing to spend $3,000 to get that new customer?

According to Principle #1 above, absolutely! Then, according to Principle #2, you're next question should be, how can you do this more often, right?

The good news is that you're not going to have to pay $3,000 every time to get a new customer. Sometimes it will be $356, sometimes $1,972, and other times $894, or whatever.

In fact, I was speaking with a doctor recently and it was his goal to spend no more than $100 to get a new patient. It turns out the reason why was because he could buy a limited number of new patient leads from a company at this amount. This is an absurd way of thinking. Here's why:

Let's say your average new customer is equal to $2,000 in profit. If all your competitors were of the mindset that they were only going to spend $100 to acquire a new customer, but you were willing to spend $800, who do you think is going to be more successful at acquiring the new customers?

Naturally, you would!

This concept is so important to understand because it will allow you to horde all the new customers you can. It will also drive your competition absolutely nuts because they'll see you crushing it but won't be able to see how you're doing it.

Remember, half of something is better then 100% of nothing. In this case, $1,200 in profit is better than no profit.

As you'll soon come to discover while reading the rest of this book, this is the power of inbound marketing!

Chapter 2

7 Ways Inbound Marketing Pays

You may be asking, is inbound marketing really all that profitable?

I'm glad you asked.

When done correctly, here are 7 ways inbound marketing can mean big payouts for you and your business:

#1: Lower Costs = Higher Profits

Studies have shown that leads generated through inbound marketing cost 61% less to acquire than those generated by traditional means [State of Inbound Marketing Report, HubSpot].

What does this mean though?

Let's say your monthly marketing budget is $10,000 from which you typically generate 45 leads a month through outbound marketing methods. According to this statistic, you will get 115 leads if you invest that same budget into inbound marketing instead.

That's 255% more leads than you were generating with outbound marketing! And, if you kept your lead-to-customer conversion rate the same, your revenue would increase by that same 255%!

What's interesting is the effect this change has on your cost-per-lead. Using the same numbers above, you would see your cost-per-lead drop from $222 each to just $87.

As if that wasn't enough of a reason to implement inbound marketing this very instant, here are several other reasons:

#2: Better Search Visibility

There's a reason why in June of 2011 Google launched Google+ (also written as Google Plus). They wanted to find their way into the profitable social media space which integrates with many of their other online properties.

According to GlobalWebIndex, Google+ is the second largest social network in the world behind Facebook. Even if it's not being used as much as Facebook, Google+ is still a force to be reckoned with simply because of it's all-powerful owner.

And speaking of Facebook, it's the same reason why they have an ongoing relationship of sharing data and functionality with Bing, the second most used search engine in America.

The fine line between search and social media has become blurred. Basically, search rankings are becoming more personalized based on our social media circles and social media activities.

Simply put, social media signals are influencing the search engines. A "hermit business" can no longer survive in the search results. It's time to be social and embrace inbound marketing if you want to be visible on search engines.

#3: More Traffic, Better Traffic

As an inbound marketing expert, all too often I hear about a business who's sales have plummeted overnight because Google made a change to their system.

Casualties from such updates even include major players like eBay, About.com, MerchantCircle, and Ask.com.

They put all their eggs in one basket, so to speak. This is a dangerous way to live, or more accurately, a temporary way to live.

In contrast, this is what makes inbound marketing

so great. It's not just about getting ranked at the top of Google and getting traffic to your site from online searches. Rather, it's about increasing your visibility and driving traffic to your business from a host of other websites.

When inbound marketing is done correctly, you're diversified across many marketing channels... blogs, multiple social media profiles, video sites, etc.. If one of them changes their system and cuts you off from their referring traffic, so be it! You'll be fine because your traffic is diversified.

Only then will you stop worrying every time Google "farts" (my crude way of describing the changes Google makes to its algorithms). And in time, with inbound marketing, you'll be getting more traffic that is more solid for the future of your business.

#4: Higher Conversion Rates

Inbound marketing is about making your business more profitable. One way this can be accomplished is by increasing your conversion rates.

As an example, let's see how social media can do just that. A scientific study shows that 51% of Facebook fans are more likely to buy from a business they follow [Chadwick Martin Bailey and iModerate Research Technologies].

So, if you are actively growing your Facebook fan base and interacting with them appropriately, you will convert a much larger percentage of them into paying customers.

As you'll see in chapters 4 and 9, I'm going to share with you other ways inbound marketing can help increase conversion rates. Getting traffic to your website is one thing. Getting that traffic to buy from you is another.

#5: Improved Reputation

Chances are you've heard of the term "reputation management." If you have, hopefully it's not because your reputation has been attacked on the internet and you're now trying to repair it. These attacks can be published in a variety of formats, but often they come in the form of online reviews and complaints on websites like ripoffreport.com, complaints.com, and local directories like yelp.com.

The good news is that inbound marketing has an intrinsic benefit which naturally assists you in managing a positive online reputation.

For instance, a complete inbound marketing campaign will likely include a system for obtaining good, 5-star reviews from your customers. If and when you get a degrading 1-star review from a disgruntled customer, you'll be just fine because your review system is already in place. It's just a matter of time before that 1-star review will be buried and out of sight.

I'll go into more detail about how you can use inbound marketing to your benefit when it comes to reputation management in chapter 13.

#6: Happier Customers

The core of inbound marketing is creating exceptional, engaging content. And if you're sharing this type of content with the right audience, why wouldn't it make them happy?

Remember the Inbound Marketing Triangle? Well, when somebody finds you on Google or hears their friend rave about you on Facebook, they're more likely to buy from your business if the message on your website is on target.

Happy customers also equal more referrals and more revenue for you and your business. To that point, Facebook users are 60% more likely to recommend a business that they're a fan of [Chadwick Martin Bailey and iModerate Research Technologies].

#7: Make More Money

Again, a reason you should be doing inbound marketing is that it will increase your revenue.

Lower cost leads, better search visibility, more traffic, better traffic, higher conversion rates, improved reputation and happy customers together will exponentially produce more sales.

You're in business for a reason, and it's surely not to lose money. (If you ask me, the federal government has that covered for all of us.)

The more money you have...

...the more vacations you can take...

...the more employees you can hire...

...the more donations you can give...

...the more secure your retirement will be...

...the more people you can help...

I could go on and on, but you get the point. Let inbound marketing help you make more money so you can do more good with it, for you and other people.

That's what this section is all about. Whether you do it yourself or hire a professional team like the one I currently manage, you're going to discover how to best implement the Inbound Marketing Triangle.

Chapter 3

Has Your Marketing Changed With The Times?

According to Wikipedia, the encyclopedia for our day and age, inbound marketing is defined as follows:

Marketing that earns the attention of customers, makes the company easy to be found, and draws customers to the website by producing interesting content.

I like this definition and agree with it wholeheartedly. However, to really understand what inbound marketing is, you first have to uncover the differences between inbound and outbound marketing. Chances are, you're more familiar with the latter.

True Story

There's a pair of doctors at this one practice near my home town. Before they became a customer of ours a couple of years ago they were already doing quite a bit of advertising on the radio, billboards, the internet, the whole shebang.

Here's the thing though... They already had a website and were buying a bunch of online marketing with another company, a direct competitor of ours.

So there I was, having a conversation with both doctors and their office manager. They were drilling me with questions and it quickly became apparent that they were not very open minded.

Why do you think this was?

It turns out that they were paying a marketing company gobs of money but the results just weren't there. They ran the type of operation where they weren't very good at getting work done on time or returning phone calls as promptly as they were at sending invoices!

The office manager, and especially the doctors, really didn't have an idea of the return they were getting for their money. After looking into their reports we determined that they were generating just a few thousand dollars of revenue from the internet each year.

That's not a typo! Yes, they spent thousands and

thousands of dollars for just a few thousand in return.

(What is a new customer worth to you? Remember, you're not in business to break even or support other companies.)

And so that was the situation I walked into a couple of years ago. These doctors were at a crossroads and were deciding which path they would take... to stay with their current marketing company or work with us.

As you could guess, they made the smart decision. To this day we're still working together. Why is this dental practice so happy though? Because last year their practice generated about $260,000 from the internet. In reality, the inbound marketing techniques we we're implementing for them are working like gang busters!

Maybe $260,000 a year does not sound like a lot to you in your business. But here's the thing... It doesn't matter as long as the marketing is as profitable as it can be, right? In this case, their return on investment is outstanding!

Times... They're A-Changin'

Whenever I was given a report assignment as a kid in elementary school, I didn't have the internet to turn to for my research. If you're like me, you went to the bookshelf and pulled out one of the hard covered encyclopedias.

And if our set of World Book Encyclopedias weren't sufficient, I hopped in the car with my mom and brothers for a special trip to the city's public library downtown.

This was before Caller I.D. and cell phones. Before the internet and, of course, before Google. Back then our telephones had cords and dial tones and TV's were virtually square!

Need to look up a phone number for a business? Just a few years ago we didn't pull out our smartphones and "google it." No, we likely went to the kitchen cupboard, pulled out a tattered phone book and flipped through its yellow pages.

It seems like the only time I handle a phone book anymore is to pick up the freshly printed copies left on my front doorstep and drop them in the blue recycle bin.

Then there's our cell phones. Remember when we used to use them for just making phone calls? I look back an laugh that my first one was a "brick phone" for which I paid $30 a month for a whopping 75 minutes.

Times were simpler then, right?

Today instead of the phone book, we often turn to websites like Google or Yelp. Our sets of World Book Encyclopedias have been replaced the virtual and relatively inferior Wikipedia. Our cell phones have been replaced by smartphones on which we can talk, email, chat, socialize, play games, surf the internet and do just about everything else except fry an egg (I'm certain that's coming too).

Frankly, your marketing methods need to evolve as well. You can't just blindly place an ad on television or in the yellow pages and hope it brings new business through the door. These days, marketing has become much more complicated and takes much more effort. At the same time, I believe it's become much more profitable.

In the following chapters, you're going to discover tactical methods of how inbound marketing can help you do just that.

Chapter 4

Inbound vs. Outbound Marketing

Inbound marketing is a term that hasn't been around for very many years. To give you some perspective, it's worthwhile to compare it to outbound marketing.

Here is a list of examples of mostly internet-based inbound marketing channels:

- Blogs
- Social Media
- Networking
- Online Videos
- Opt-In Forms
- eNewsletters
- Podcasts
- Seminars
- Whitepapers
- eBooks
- Search Engine Optimization

By contrast, outbound marketing encompasses more traditional methods of getting the word out:

- Newspaper ads
- Yellow page ads
- Direct mail
- Billboards and signs
- Radio spots
- TV commercials
- Outbound sales

One reason inbound marketing is appealing is because outbound marketing is becoming increasingly more expensive and often difficult to implement these days.

Marketing really has changed! Take a look at the table on the right.

Inbound vs. Outbound: Communication

One of the major differences between inbound and outbound marketing is the lines of communication.

Outbound marketing is typically one-way. For example, when you're watching a television commercial you can't respond to that advertisement and have a discussion with it. Admittedly, I talk to my TV when I'm watching football (and my kids make fun of me for it), but still, my words are not being received, making it just a one-way conversation.

On the other hand, two-way communication is the essence of inbound marketing! If you write a blog post your audience can likely respond with a comment or share it on their social networks. Speaking of social

Then	Now
TV Commercials	DVRs, YouTube, Streaming Video
Telemarketing	No Call Lists
Email Solicitations	FCC Ban, Spam Filters
Direct Mail	Annual Postage Rate Increases
Radio Commercials	MP3 Players, Podcasts, Pandora, Spotify
Automated Dialer Phone Calls	FCC Ban
Door-To-Door Sales	No Soliciting Signs, Webinars
Phone Book Ads	Google, Local Online Directories
Newspaper and Magazine Ads	Online Versions, Reduced Subscriber Bases
Books	eBooks, eReaders
Trade Shows	Webinars, Increased Cost of Travel

networks, how can they be considered "social" if they didn't provide a way to have back-and-forth conversations?

Inbound vs. Outbound: Duration

I don't subscribe to the newspaper anymore, but when I did they were usually thrown in the recycle bin by the next day. At the same time, all the ads printed in those paper were discarded, never to be seen again. What a waste, right?

As a general rule, outbound marketing is temporary. As soon as you stop paying for that billboard, any and all leads generated by it come to a screeching halt. Your direct mail piece is unable to produce leads unless you send out another batch. Radio commercials can only be heard as long as the invoices for them are being paid.

I equate outbound marketing to my kitchen faucet. It can only generate leads (water) when I have it turned on. Inbound marketing, however, is more like the rivers here in Idaho. Leads (water) are always flowing!

If you write and publish an interesting post on your blog, it will always be there unless you take it down. The same goes for videos you upload to sites like YouTube and your business listings on online directories.

Of course, there are some exceptions to the rule, but inbound marketing content is typically longer lasting compared to outbound marketing content.

Inbound vs. Outbound: Interruption

Commercials interrupt television shows. Billboards interrupt scenic views. Telemarketing calls interrupt family dinners.

Other experts refer to outbound marketing as

"interruption marketing." I can see their point of view, but don't agree that outbound marketing is always interrupting.

Take our direct mail newsletter as an example. We often get feedback from subscribers who tell us they appreciate the content we provide in the newsletter. Some of them like it so much that they save each issue and store them in a 3-ring binder.

I doubt very much that they see our direct mail newsletter as an interruption! (Maybe this is because our newsletter is closer to the inbound side of things as opposed to outbound.)

Anyway, inbound marketing cannot be confused as interruption marketing when done correctly. In fact, it's more like "get found marketing."

Inbound vs. Outbound: Other

While inbound channels are fresh and evolving, outbound channels tend to be antiquated. Look at what Google has done to phone books, what Craigslist has done to newspaper classifieds, and what Amazon has done to K-Mart.

With outbound marketing, the focus is often on the company, its product, or how great it is. Inbound marketing focuses more on educating, entertaining, and informing the prospect.

Finally, new customers are sought-out and sold

to through outbound marketing while inbound marketing naturally attracts the customers. The major benefit here is how the company is positioned during the sales process. Ask yourself, would you rather chase the customers or be chased by them?

Stop Outbound Marketing?

To avoid any confusion, at Inbound Systems we still believe in and actually use outbound marketing methods.

The book you're reading is available in print, is it not?

It's just that inbound marketing is becoming more important and effective compared to outbound marketing. Really, implementing both in conjunction with each other is ideal.

Here's an example of a marketing funnel to show how this might work.

Step 1: Direct Mail

You send a piece of direct mail to a list of qualified prospects. Instead of a call-to-action like "Buy Now" or "Call Today," you direct them back to your website for a free eBook that solves a problem.

Step 2: eNewsletter

Since they're not ready to buy right away, you

maintain contact with them through a monthly eNewsletter. The content of the eNewsletter is simply a summary of the past month's blog posts.

Step 3: Blog

One of the topics peaks your prospect's interest. So, they click on the link in the email and are redirected back to your blog to finish reading the interesting article.

Step 4: Whitepaper

At the end of your blog post is another call-to-action for a free analysis. It happens to relate to the topic of the exact post they just read so they opt-in. During the analysis you pitch your sale but unfortunately they don't buy just yet.

Step 5: Social Media & Reviews

What you said was interesting to your prospect so they research your company online. They check out your social media profiles and reputation on review websites. Your company passes the test and they call you to complete the sale.

There you have it! A perfectly good example of how to enhance your outbound marketing strategy (direct mail) with inbound marketing strategies (eBook, eNewsletter, blog, whitepaper, social media).

Using the example above, without the follow up, engaging content, and positive online reputation, you may have lost this buyer forever. This is why it's important to diversify your marketing efforts and make sure you're utilizing a wide variety of inbound marketing tactics at the same time.

Chapter 5

The Inbound Marketing Triangle

If you follow the master of direct-response marketing, Dan Kennedy, you'll be familiar with his Direct Marketing Triangle:

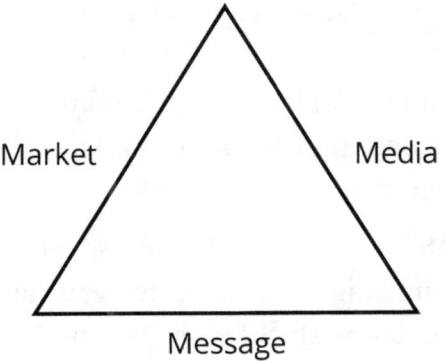

The concept above is about creating the right content (Message), for the right people (Market), then putting it in the right places (Media).

It's a basic theory. So, for example, if your primary target market is teenagers, you're probably going to be using a grandpa in your TV commercial and air it on the Disney channel.

Inbound marketing is no different, which is why I came up with what I call the Inbound Marketing Triangle.

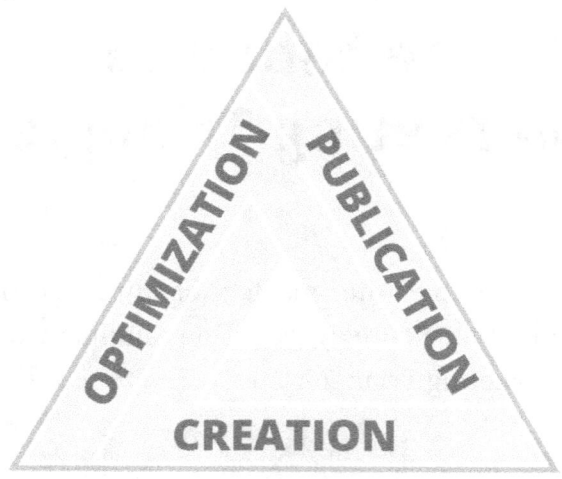

First, content. I placed it on the bottom because it is the foundation of inbound marketing. It's very important and it has to be done right.

The optimization side is almost as important. Without optimizing the content for your audience, it will not resonate with them or be found online (i.e. Google).

What good is the optimized content if you don't place it where your audience can consume it? The publication side of the triangle illustrates the need for distributing your content in strategic locations.

Each of the three parts are vital to the success of an inbound marketing campaign. Without one, the other two will likely fail, just as a three-legged table will fall when you take a leg away.

In the following three chapters I'm going to dive into each of these sides of the triangle so you can get the most out of inbound marketing.

Chapter 6

Why Your Content Should Be CRAP

Perhaps you have heard the saying, "Content is king." Well, as cliché as it may be, this statement is true!

Inbound marketing is NOTHING without quality content. And by quality I'm talking about engaging articles, videos, photos and posts that are shareable, likeable, interactable, and worthy of a conversation.

That's a lot to take in, so in a word, the content you create for inbound marketing purposes must be CRAP.

What? CRAP?

Yes, I said CRAP, but not in the way you're thinking!

I'm a graphic designer by trade, and way back in

school I was taught the design principles of CRAP. It's actually an acronym...

>**C**ontrast
>**R**epetition
>**A**lignment
>**P**roximity

Ironically, CRAP design is good design. These principles also apply to good inbound marketing content. Here's how...

Contrast

According to WorldWideWebSize.com, there are at least 3.6 billion pages on the indexed web. Regardless of how many web pages there are, it's easy to get lost as a business on the internet if you don't set yourself apart from the crowd.

This is where contrast comes into play. The goal is to be different, be a nonconformist, be contrasting so that you can garner the attention of your target audience.

Allow me to show you 5 ways to implement contrast when it comes to your content:

#1: Sense of Humor

Are you in a serious industry? Be appropriately funny when your competitors are scared to. I'll give you an example...

WHY YOUR CONTENT SHOULD BE CRAP

We have a customer who owns and operates a prominent alcohol and drug treatment center. Serious stuff, right? For a post on one of the social media accounts we help manage for them, we took a chance and presented the following meme:

To our surprise, our customer loved it and said to go forward with posting it. We did and the meme got a positive response with no backlash. We were able to insert a bit of light on an otherwise dark subject.

#2: Free Advice

Who doesn't like getting something for free? When your competitors are charging for advice, don't be afraid to give it out freely on the internet. You can do this through extended blog articles, free whitepapers, or tidbits of information on social media posts.

One of our customers is a national interior design firm and most of their competition is hesitant to give out design tips and advice without first collecting a fee. Our customer had the right idea though. They understood that if somebody is going to take their free advice and not hire them because of it, they were more likely a do-it-yourselfer and not their target client anyway!

If you have a scarcity mindset like this customer's competitors, now is the time to change your thinking. Set yourself apart from the competition and start giving away your secrets. Take it from Ralph Waldo Emerson who said,

"It is one of the most beautiful compensations of this life that no man can sincerely try to help another without helping himself."

#3: Awesome Design

There are companies out there that provide niche websites for their target industries. The dental niche is plagued with these types of sites and the problem is that all the designs seem very similar. Even more, the text is all the same with every website, except for a few pages.

What value does this provide to the prospective dental patient? When they're searching on Google for a new dentist and they see the same website over and over again, how boring is that?

If you find yourself in this scenario, it will be easy for you to contrast your business from the competition. Invest in a new website with a custom design and unique content if you must. Ask yourself, what can you do to WOW your audience the moment they arrive on your website? Not only will you stand out, but it will also help you in converting internet traffic into new customers or patients.

#4: Variety of Topics

Since we all understand visiting the dentist, let's continue with the dental theme. If all you do is blog and post about dentistry, again, how boring is that? Mix up your posts with off-topic content that is engaging and interesting to your prospective audience.

I'll give you some ideas for content later on in chapter 11, but the point to be understood now is to make sure that there's contrast within the topics of your content. Otherwise, your content might fall on deaf ears and your efforts may go to waste.

#5: Text, Images and Videos

Which single type of content should you post for inbound marketing purposes: text, images, or videos? The answer is, all of the above.

Yes, statistics show that images perform handsomely on social media platforms like Facebook when compared to plain text posts. However, if you only posted images, complacency may take over with your audience's attention.

It's ideal to use a variety of posts... some with just text, others with videos, and others with images.

Repetition

The second principle of CRAP content is repetition. It can be a tough balance because on the surface repetition may seem like an antonym of contrast. For good content though, you have to maintain repetition and contrast at the same time.

As an example, we have a customer who heads a real estate investment firm. Since we help him with his blogging and social media, we came up with an idea to spotlight one of his investments on a monthly basis.

His name is David and so we called the series David's Deal of the Month. As silly as it may sound, two words that start with the same letter, an alliteration, gives this title a nice, memorable ring to it!

More importantly though, having a topic that we can address on a monthly basis makes it easier to create that content, while at the same time giving the audience a reason to revisit the site regularly.

I've seen this done in a number of different ways and formats:

- **Healthy Tip Tuesday:** A weekly Facebook post

that shares just one useful health tip.

- **Obscure Holiday of the Month:** An interesting off-topic post that highlights a not so well known holiday.
- **Strategy Saturday:** A weekly two to three minute video that gives free instruction and education.
- **Customer Spotlights:** This is usually good for monthly or quarterly blog posts. Employees can also be spotlighted.
- **Money Saving Mondays:** Weekly emails to a subscriber list of people who want to save money.
- **Wordless Wednesdays:** Like they say, pictures can say a thousand words! This is the posting of just a image, and you got it, no words. The goal is simply to provoke thought and comments.

Alignment

With graphic design, alignment of every element needs to be placed on purpose and in-line with the other elements. The same goes for your content. It needs to be created and placed in the right locations on purpose.

Don't post to Facebook just to be able to say that you do social media. Don't just post a photo to Flickr because you just have to get something up on your profile. Don't do search engine optimization just because you want number 1 rankings on Google.

Instead, you should ask yourself questions like these when it comes to your content:

- Is Facebook the right platform to convey my message or should it be a blog post?
- Would my audience share or like this topic?
- Is my audience active on LinkedIn?
- Am I creating content that is 100% original or presented in a unique fashion?
- Is my audience going to enjoy this content or find it interesting?
- Would I post this content if there was no Google?

When you align your content with what your audience wants and needs, this portion of CRAP will be satisfied... just like your audience will be satisfied when the consume it!

Proximity

Finally, the last principle of CRAP is proximity. In graphic design, proximity is the way elements are organized in relation to the other elements. Again, this is done on purpose, and with content, it's no different.

To apply this principle to a blog post, as an example, you're going to want to make sure the title is dialed in. And by dialed in, I mean so interesting that your audience will have no choice but to read the blog post. Think about it for a sec. If you don't find the headline of a magazine article interesting, are you likely to read it? Probably not! (This topic is so important that I'll be diving into it in greater detail in chapter 11.)

That's not where it stops either. The first few paragraphs of the blog post have to be just as engaging. Do this by placing the most interesting part, the most intriguing story, or the most controversial point of view at the front of the blog post. Otherwise, if you place it in the middle or the end, the post may never get read at all!

Proximity also applies to how your web pages are laid out. If you have an opt-in form (and you should), place it on the pages and in the spots that convert the best. In the header or just about anywhere above the fold works.

Effective search engine optimization incorporates proximity as well. Where you place the keywords you're targeting in your content needs to be done purposefully. Just be careful though. If you overdo it, you may get penalized by Google for "over optimizing" your web pages. You'll want to make sure there is balance between your content making sense for your audience and being optimized for Google.

There you have it... You now know what I truly mean by creating content that's CRAP! In chapter 11 I'll be getting into more detail about specific methods of creating CRAP content. In the meantime, the next side of the Inbound Marketing Triangle is optimization.

Chapter 7

A Surprising Approach to Optimization

With the title of this chapter being what it is, your first instincts may be that I'm referring to search engine optimization, or SEO for short.

Yes and no.

I don't think that I could stress this idea enough, but your audience comes first, Google second... and this includes the optimization of your content!

How to Optimize for Your Audience

Ideally, you should know who your audience is before writing an article, posting a photo or uploading a video. Once the content has been created though, you'll want to double-check that it appeals to the interests of your target market. What you want to do here is define who exactly your audience is. Doing so will actually make it easier to create the content in the first place.

So, who is your target market? It seems like a general question, but it's best to get down to specifics here. And what you want to do is think of your audience on an individual basis, not as a group.

Decision Makers vs. Influencers

To fully understand your audience you need to first separate the influencers from decision makers. For instance, if you sell kids clothes, often the child will be an influencer and the parent the decision maker. If you sell to medical offices, the office manager may be the influencer and the doctor the decision maker. In corporate environments, a board of advisors may be the decision maker and the CEO the influencer.

You'll have to come to this conclusion on your own, but let's look at this a little deeper!

If you sell supplies to chiropractors, the office manager is often the decision maker when it comes to first introducing your products to the doctor. At that point, the doctor is the decision maker and the office manager is the influencer.

Complicated? Yeah.

Am I over thinking it? Maybe a bit.

I just wanted to expose you to the idea that there

are multiple steps and decision makers along the way. As a result, you may need to tailor your content appropriately.

Demographics vs. Psychographics

You've heard of demographics before. They classify who your decision makers are, right? Well, they're important and need to be specified prior to creating your content.

Here are some key demographics to consider:

- Gender
- Age Range
- Location
- Language Spoken
- Occupation or Title
- Income

This is all data that you might find in a census report. It helps, but this data has its limitations, which brings me to psychographics. I would argue that these are much more important than demographics.

Here are some key psychographics to consider:

- Beliefs
- Desires
- Attitudes
- Interests
- Fears

Defining your target market's psychographics will allow you to create content that really resonates with them. Why? Because they'll feel that you really understand them, and as a result, they will trust, follow, and recommend you more.

So, let's uncover the psychographics of your decision makers with a series of questions. (Truth be told, I can't claim to have developed the following questions because they've been published elsewhere multiple times over. And, I don't know who to give credit for them just because I've heard them from several different sources.)

Keep in mind that all the answers to these questions should be relative to what you sell:

- What problem can you solve for your decision maker?
- What concerns keep your decision maker awake at night, trouble-minded and staring at the ceiling?
- What is your decision maker afraid of?
- Who is the enemy of your decision maker?
- How would your decision maker finish this sentence: "If I could just _____."
- What are the habits of your decision maker?

Basically, you're a problem solver here! Your prospect has some sort of issue, and you, with your product or service, can resolve it.

If they don't have a problem, then they're not your prospect and you should move on to the next prospect. See how simple this is?

Remember, Google isn't buying your stuff here.

A SURPRISING APPROACH TO OPTIMIZATION

So, everything you do for inbound marketing should benefit YOUR AUDIENCE in some way, large or small. Above all, optimize your content for your audience first. Then, the search engine optimization will naturally follow.

Next up is Publication, the final side of the Inbound Marketing Triangle.

Chapter 8

Getting Published The Easy Way

Now that you've created your content and it's optimized, it needs to be published for your audience to consume.

Fortunately there is no shortage of places to get published online:

- Your Website
- Blog
- Opt-In Email
- Lead Magnets
- Social Media Profiles
- Online Directories
- Video Portals
- 3rd Party Websites

The list above can be divided into two groups. The first are online properties that you have ownership of or direct control over.

Your website, blog, and social media profile pages

would fall into this category. And since you control these types of properties, you typically have full control over the content that's published.

The second type are web pages that you don't own or have direct control over. This includes 3rd party websites such as other blogs, online article sites, news portals, association websites, and other industry or geographically niche websites.

Although getting published on a website that you don't control is a bit more challenging, it can be even more rewarding. Doing so will not only help you to fall into favor with search engines like Google, but you'll also expand your online reach and increase your overall visibility (I cover these benefits and strategies in chapter 15).

Where you get published online actually depends on your niche and audience. Basically, you're going to want to get published on sites where your audience is already hanging out online.

So, survey your best customers and ask them questions pertinent to your content:

- Which social media platforms and search engines do they use?
- What content format do they prefer? (articles, short snippits, video)
- When are they online and active with their social media profiles?

- Do they have an email address?

As you take all this into consideration when publishing your optimized content you'll see increased engagement and a better return on your inbound marketing investment.

You'll also want to cater your publishing strategy based on your type of business. For instance:

- If you're a local business, you'll want to make sure you're visible on 100's of local directories.
- If you're a large manufacturer, getting published on vendor websites may be beneficial.
- If you're a celebrity in your niche or you hold conferences and events, Twitter can be a useful publishing tool.

No matter what industry you're in, there are places to get published that I consider mandatory. Your website, blog, opt-in email, and social media are important for any company's inbound marketing campaign.

That wraps up the three sides of the Inbound Marketing Triangle. Now, let's dive into the more tactical side of inbound marketing!

Chapter 9

Have a Website You Can Be Proud Of

A fully optimized and effective website is so important, that I consider it the hub of any profitable inbound marketing campaign.

Here are four quick tips for having a website that you can be proud of:

Tip #1: Get One

Since you're reading this book about inbound marketing, you likely have a website already. But if you operate a small business, the odds are not in your favor. In fact, Google did a study with Ipsos and found that 58% of U.S. small businesses do not have a website.

Why should you get a website in the first place? A

recent BCG Report called, *The Connected World: The $4.2 Trillion Opportunity,* showed that over the next 3 years, businesses that make use of the web expect to grow 40% faster than those that don't.

Simply put, it comes down to growing your business and making more money. If that isn't a compelling reason to get a website, I don't know what is.

Tip #2: Good-Enough Design

You don't need the world's most spectacular website either. A website that is good enough is just that, good enough.

Remember the CRAP acronym I used earlier in regards to your content? Whenever possible the same principles need to apply to the design of your website.

Contrast

Be sure the areas of your website are well defined but cohesive with one another. This includes taking a look at your header, navigation, content area, sidebar content and footer.

Repetition

It's important to repeat colors, shapes, lines and styles and to keep them consistent. Otherwise your website will appear hodgepodge and confusing.

Alignment

The elements of your website need to be placed on purpose and in line with the other elements. Each element should appear visually connected with everything else.

Proximity

The way elements are grouped together, spaced apart, and organized in relation to the other elements should also be considered.

Your competent web developer can take care of these updates for you since you now know what to ask for.

Tip #3: Responsiveness & Organization

The way the content on your website is structured is also something important to consider. If the content is intuitively functional, then your visitors will view more pages and stay longer on your site, increasing the likelihood that they'll purchase your products or services.

What do I mean by functional? Here's a few things to consider:

Responsive Design

These days, nearly 2/3 of people access the internet on their cell phones while over 1/3 own tablets. We are no longer in a desktop-only internet world! This is why it's vital to make your website mobile ready. The ideal way of doing so is with a responsively designed website as opposed to a separate mobile site.

A responsive website is a single site that automatically adapts and responds to how it's displayed based on the device the user is viewing it on. So, if you're looking at your website on your smartphone, there wouldn't be a need to pinch the screen to zoom in and out or to scroll left and right to read the text.

Besides being more user friendly, responsive websites are also preferred by Google.

Universal Navigation

A single menu that lists all the major pages on the site is accessible on every single page. An alternative for large sites is to include a breadcrumb navigation, which is a trail of links for the pages visited.

Contact Information

Make it easy for your visitors to connect with you via readily available contact forms and information.

For instance, buttons that direct to your social media profiles should be visible. Also, your contact information and other details should be formatted with Schema markup. Schema is a technical method of displaying information in a manner the search engines will understand. This type of thing should be taken care of by a knowledgable developer.

The F Pattern

Eye tracking research from the Nielsen Norman Group shows that when visitors land on a website, they typically scan the content in an F-shaped pattern, two horizontal movements followed by one vertical movement on the left. Try to strategically place your calls-to-action and content based on this F pattern.

Tip #4: KISS

Perhaps you've heard of the KISS acronym... Keep It Simple, Stupid. Well, your website is not exempt if you want it to be as effective as it can be.

Yes, it's good to maintain simplicity with your site's design, but it also applies to your content. For instance, it's not necessary to publish a page for every single concept in regards to your business. I actually think this type of content is more appropriate for the topics of your blog posts.

The main pages of your website should answer just the overall points of interest for your visitors. In this case, less is more!

Chapter 10

How to Ethically Manipulate Google

I believe if you've truly optimized the content for your audience first, then it's pretty much optimized for search engines like Google already. At this point it's just a matter of fine-tuning and making sure you don't get blacklisted or penalized by the search engines.

Search engine optimization, or SEO for short, is the practice of making your content more friendly to the search engines. As long as it doesn't hurt the user experience or contradict Google's webmaster guidelines, I view search engine optimization as a way to ethically manipulate Google. Here are some of my suggestions:

For DIY'ers:

If you tend to be a do-it-yourselfer (whether yourself or a non-expert employee) that's okay. I just don't think it's a good thing when it comes to optimizing your content.

First, you currently have enough to worry about. And since Google updates their search algorithm (how they calculate their search results) about 50 times a month, it's difficult to keep up with the latest releases. Really, you could end up doing more harm than good.

This brings me to my second point. Unless you have extensive experience with SEO, it's difficult to know which strategies are legit or not. The reality is, if you unknowingly do something that is against Google's guidelines, it could land you a penalty that results in a drop in traffic to your site.

Okay, I'll step off my soap box now and give you some pointers on how to keep your professional SEO company in check...

Forget the Easy Button

First, let me just say that Google is smart. By smart, I mean really, really, really smart. And because of this, there are no shortcuts when it comes to optimizing your content for Google.

The reason is, if you try to find a loophole and

trick Google to increase the search engine traffic to your site, chances are they're already aware of that loophole and have either resolved it or are in the process of resolving it.

To provide an ideal and exceptional experience for its users, Google is constantly cracking down on low quality content. In fact, they have an entire department called the Webspam team devoted solely to hunting down and penalizing offenders.

How do they do this? Through updates to their search algorithm like Hummingbird.

Meet Hummingbird

Google names each of it's major updates. Among the most recent ones are Panda, Penguin, and now Hummingbird. It's almost like Google has it's own zoo!

Perhaps you've heard of, or worse, been negatively effected by these updates.

With each new release, Google aims to improve its search results and weed out the low quality stuff. To illustrate just how intelligent Google's algorithm has become, I'll give you an example...

Let's say you're at home getting ready for a short business trip to Chicago. Although your time there is tight, you want to make sure you experience an authentic, deep-dish, Chicago pizza topped with real

Italian beef sausage. Since you're not from Chicago, where do you turn when planning your little excursion? The internet of course! More specifically, statistics show that you'd likely turn to Google.

So, you open up your internet browser and type "best pizza in Chicago" into a Google search. The results that appear next on your screen are not by accident.

You see, with the Hummingbird update, each word you type in the search box matters. Google no longer takes just the words "pizza" and "Chicago" into consideration like they used to.

The word "in" tells Google that you're looking for a pizza restaurant with a Chicago address. Location matters here because if you didn't include the word "in" you might just get restaurants in your own city that sell Chicago-style pizza because your computer is not in Chicago (yes, Google knows approximately where your computer is located). Or, Google may show you recipes for Chicago-style pizza.

See the difference here? It's a small but relatively significant concept that Google will take into consideration when determining the search results you see.

Now let's take a look at the word "best" in the search phrase. In this case, Google figures that you don't want a stale Chicago style pizza that tastes like cardboard. No, you want the best, right? But how in the world can Google tell if a pizza is delicious or not? From it's reviews, of course! Through Google+ profiles, Google's users rate the pizza places they've been to in Chicago and give them a score.

Based on all this data and literally hundreds of other factors, Google can give you a good idea of where to find the best pizza in Chicago.

SIDE NOTE: This is just one reason why focusing on a few keywords and where you rank on Google are becoming less and less relevant. Sure, if you operate a pizza restaurant you could rank number one for the "Chicago pizza" keyword. But, using my example above, if you don't have a Chicago address or lots of positive online reviews, your number one ranking means squat! It's best to just focus on publishing high quality, optimized content in the right places and forget about search rankings.

What NOT To Do

Of course, there are strategies you'll want to avoid when it comes to optimization. If you do you'll also avoid triggering a penalty from Google.

#1: Duplicate Content:

As far as Google is concerned, do you think they're going to give better visibility to a website that has the same content as hundreds of other sites, or to the single website that publishes original content that cannot be found anywhere else on the web? If you didn't create your website content in-house, there's a good chance it's not original and was copied from either vendor collateral or other websites designed by your web developer.

#2: Keyword Stuffing

This is the practice of placing keywords in places they don't need to be placed. When we're auditing another company's optimization work, we often see this type of over-optimization. This includes stuffing keywords into page titles, meta descriptions, keywords meta tag (which shouldn't be used at all), image alt tags, and page text.

Perhaps you've visited a website and they use the same few words over and over again to the point where it just seems weird. Well, this is likely a sign of over-optimization and often results in a poor user experience.

#3: Buying Links

You may already be aware of this, but getting other quality websites to link to yours is a great strategy for increasing your online visibility. Just be careful though. You don't want to buy links or hire an optimization company who says they're doing link building for you when in actuality they're just buying links on your behalf.

When it comes to optimization, a good rule of thumb to follow is to ask yourself the following question:

If there was no such thing as Google, would I _____ ?

The answers then become clear:

No, you're not going to have duplicate content because it also creates a subpar user experience.

No, you're not going to stuff keywords in places they wouldn't make sense to the user.

No, you're not going to want that link because it is coming from an irrelevant website.

You see, manipulating Google really isn't about Google in the first place. It's about your audience, the people who are actually able to make the purchase.

Chapter 11

Blogging Your Way to Profits

A blog on your website is the ideal place to provide fresh and interesting content to your audience.

What is a blog? It's a shortened word for a web log. Originally they were utilized as online journals, and I guess you can say they still are. You control the content and publish it whenever you like.

If you're not familiar to the blog-o-sphere, you may be wondering why your company should host and maintain a blog.

Studies show that companies that blog get 97% more links to their website compared to companies that don't blog. In reality, the more websites that link to yours, the more traffic you'll get.

This contributes to the fact that companies that blog also get 55% more traffic than those that don't. Isn't that what you'd like... more traffic to your website?

And finally, if you blog, studies show that on average you're going to get 70% more leads than your competitors who don't blog.

One reason why you may experience all these benefits comes down to a simple numbers game.

For search engines to send you traffic, they have to know about your website, right? Well, the more blog posts you create, the more pages your website will have for the search engines to index. And more indexed pages means you are likely to see more links, traffic, and leads.

Get Famous!

Want another compelling reason why you should blog?

When you're reading a book or published article, how do you perceive the author of that publication? Unless they're a total idiot, you likely view that person as an expert. On some level, you may even look up to them as a celebrity when it comes to their published topic.

The same goes for you and your blog. As long as your content is high quality stuff, then others will look to you as an expert and possibly a celebrity.

Multi-Personalities

If you don't like the term blog, that's perfectly fine. We've had customers who felt the same way. The simple solution is to still maintain a blog, but call it something else:

- Weekly Update
- Daily Dose
- News Releases
- Articles
- Q&A
- Library

Okay, so now that you see why your company needs a blog, let's dive into exactly how to go about implementing one.

Solutions Based Writing

First, understand that your goal with blogging should aim to solve problems that are being experienced by your audience. I'm not just referring to problems they have that are solved by your products or services. You have to think broader than that.

What other issues do they face on a day to day basis that you can speak to in an educated manner? Whatever topic you choose to blog about, be helpful FIRST.

And even though your products or services may actually solve their problems, you don't want to use your blog as a platform for selling. I'm not saying that you can't blog about your products and services (by all means, you should!). You just don't want to sell them from your blog posts. That part comes later!

Your Audience Comes First

What I mean by this is that you should create content for your prospects and the visitors to your website as opposed to search engines like Google.

A good question to ask yourself again is, would you create the blog post if there was no such thing as Google? True, search engines like Google may be a large source of traffic for your website, but that shouldn't be the sole reason you're blogging.

Look at it this way... If Google sends you traffic and your website is not compelling for your audience, they're not going to buy from you. Then, the resources you put into those blog posts have just gone to waste.

So, when writing for your audience, be sure to focus on them and include information that is engaging and interesting from their point of view. Depending on your blog post, this may include statistics, data, tips and best practices.

10 Blog Topic Ideas

One of the many reasons companies hire our writers at Inbound Systems to write their blog content is because the companies cannot generate interesting enough content in a cost effective manner.

If this is something you struggle with as well, use the ideas below as fodder for your articles. Be creative and also come up with your own! Remember, in no way, shape, or form is the following a comprehensive list of blog topic ideas.

Idea #1: Problems

I've already covered the premise behind this idea. Now, here is the tactic... List your customers biggest problems on a piece of paper and tackle each one by providing them with a solution in a blog post.

Idea #2: Keywords

I'm not a big fan of focusing on where you rank in the search engines because I believe that good rankings will come naturally if you do inbound marketing properly. That being said, go ahead and list all the keywords you'd like to rank #1 for on Google. Then, place the similar keywords in groups and write a blog post about each group's topic.

Idea #3: News Jacking

I love this tactic! If there is something in the news that has even the smallest relation to your industry, get to the computer as fast as humanly possible and blog about it. This is a great way to ride the coattails of the media.

And if you can contribute significantly enough to

the conversation, it may not be a bad idea to distribute an optimized press release about it as well.

Idea #4: Notebook

As you go about your daily business, blogging ideas are bound to randomly pop up in your mind. When this occurs, don't let that thought fade! Write it down in a notebook or record it in a designated document on your computer.

I'm constantly coming up with unique ideas for the content we create for our customers. In fact, I do this so often that one of the writers in my office opened up a shared document called "Brodie's Brain Farts" so that she could record the random ideas that I regularly throw her way.

Idea #5: FAQ's

Whenever a customer asks you or your staff a question, write it down. Your notebook or computer document that I mentioned in the tactic #4 is a good place! With each question, you now have a new blog post idea.

Idea #6: Customer Spotlight

How would you like to duplicate your best customers? You can, but first you need to understand the ones you already have!

So here's the idea... Ask your customers if you

could spotlight them on your website. Then, either interview them in person or over the phone. Or, email them a list of questions they can answer at their leisure. Now you have the outline for an incredibly unique blog post that will likely be interesting to prospects who are similar to the customer you spotlighted.

Idea #7: Employee Spotlight

We have a company for whom we also spotlight employees on a regular basis. They have since taken this content a step further.

When they have an on-location appointment with one of their own customers, that person is emailed a link to the employee spotlight so they can become familiar with the employee beforehand. Genius right?

Idea #8: Expert Spotlight

This tactic follows the same method as above. However, the idea here is to spotlight experts and gurus who can provide added value to your audience.

As a perfect example, we did this for a customer of ours who manufacturers and sells nets of all kinds, including nets that are installed on bridges. So, we sought out a published bridge expert. We contacted him and emailed him a list of questions for the interview.

How do you think this expert responded? Well, he

wanted more publicity and to sell more of his books, didn't he?

Idea #9: Don't Press Enter

The next time you do a search on Google or Bing, type in your keyword but don't press enter. Take notice of the search terms that populate the drop down menu immediately below the keyword you just typed. These are suggested search terms coming to you free of charge from the search engine! Look through them for blog topic ideas that you may not have thought of. Then, continue to play around with it by typing various keywords.

Idea #10: Google Alerts

Get notified as it happens. Google allows you to set up a custom content alert based on the settings you provide. So, for example, if you want to be notified any time there are developments released on a niche industry website, you can set up an alert to get notified about them as they happen. Here's an example of how you might program this type of alert:

> site:nicheindustrywebsite.com "industry term"

The Secret Sauce of Blogging

Now that you have the ideas to blog about, here are some best practices when it comes to maintaining an awesome company blog. There are 9 of them.

Tactic #1: One Website

I realize this is not always possible, but it's ideal if your blog is installed on your main website instead of a separate domain. When a visitor arrive at your blog, the ultimate goal should be to convert that visitor into a paying customer. If your blog is located on your main website, the transition from visitor to paying customer is typically easier.

Tactic #2: Variety

You'll also want to mix it up when it comes to posting on your blog. Utilize a good variety of post types including articles, infographics, interviews, Q&A topics, photos, and even the embedding of videos.

Tactic #3: Rotate Authors

Depending on how large your company is, consider rotating authors in order to produce a wider variety of content.

Tactic #4: Quality vs. Length

Other experts may say you should write 400-600+ words per post. I disagree on setting a minimum length. Instead, you should only write blog posts as long as they need to be and never sacrifice quality for length. Quality comes first here.

Tactic #5: Focus

Although you should write on a wide variety of topics, my advice is to only address one topic per post. If you find yourself writing a really long blog post and veering off into a secondary topic, split it up. Now you have two or more separate articles to post.

Tactic #6: Be Consistent

How often you post depends on your niche and competition. If you're a local company, plan on posting once a week. Enterprise companies should blog anywhere from two times a week to daily. Above all, be patient and don't expect overnight results.

Tactic #7: Title

This just may be the most important aspect of a blog post. Why? Because if nobody finds your title intriguing, they're not going to read the rest of the content you wrote, right?

So, be sure your titles are interesting, beneficial, actionable, and preferably under 10 words long. Dharmesh Shah once said, "Spend half your time writing the content and half the time writing the title." These are wise words if you ask me!

Tactic #8: Calendar

If you schedule your content on a blog or content calendar, you're more likely going to produce quality content on a consistent basis. For a free content calendar template, visit the following website:

www.inboundsystems.com/contentcalendar

Tactic #9: Promote It

"If you build it, they will come" does not necessarily apply here! Once you've published your shiny-new blog post, push your engaging content on social media and via an email newsletter.

Starting and maintaining a blog may seem like a daunting task. Hopefully you've found the strategies and tactics in this chapter helpful. Of course, if you'd like help in getting awesome content regularly published on your blog, check out the solutions we offer at Inbound Systems.

Chapter 12

What You May Not Know About Email Marketing

By mentioning the term "email marketing" did I trigger thoughts in your mind of getting flagged for spam and caught by email filters? I understand if it did, but hear me out.

There's a difference between bulk email and opt-in email:

Broadcast/Bulk Email: You buy a list of emails and send out a commercial message to unsuspecting recipients without permission.

Relevant/Opt-In Email: You send emails to your own list of people who have specifically signed up to receive them from you.

See the contrast? Opt-in email is okay and a perfectly legit inbound marketing practice. It's no wonder why studies show that relevant emails drive 18 times more revenue than broadcast emails.

To illustrate how you can go about implementing it, here are two basic methods:

Method #1: Opt-In Form

In order to do opt-in email marketing, you have to have email addresses to market to, right? An opt-in form is one way of capturing those email addresses.

Let's say you've unlocked the secret to driving visitors to your website. Fantastic! However, this traffic is only valuable to you and your business *if you do something with it.*

What you need to do next is convert your visitors from prospects into leads. And if your website is optimized in this fashion, it will do just that!

True, visitors can call your office or fill out your contact form, but one of the best ways to convert your visitors into leads is what we call an opt-in form. To the right is an example of what I mean.

The basic process here is to offer your visitors something of value, typically for free, in exchange for their contact information. The thing you're giving your visitors is called a lead magnet. Offering this lead magnet allows you to make a simple connection so you can follow up with them afterwards until they buy your products or services.

Here are a handful of ideas for possible lead magnets you can utilize:

- Audio CD
- PDF report or whitepaper
- Checklist
- MP3 recording
- DVD
- Webinar invitation
- Book
- eBook
- Downloadable video

Notice how some of the lead magnets listed above are digital products (PDF, checklist, MP3 files, etc.) while others are physical products (CD, book, etc.). Offering a physical product allows you to ask for additional contact information, something you can use to your advantage in the follow up process.

Method #2: eNewsletters

A particular customer of ours at Inbound Systems has quite the story to tell when it comes to the custom eNewsletter we manage for his company. Out of the blue, the owner has emailed us a couple of times revealing the results of their campaign.

To his delight (and ours as well!), his company generated nearly $41,500 of new revenue over a three month period. He attributed it solely to the eNewsletter we managed for him and the traffic it forwarded to his website.

Amazing, right? If you have any doubt in your mind, yes, eNewsletters can be a very profitable venture!

In our experience, eNewsletters are best utilized in conjunction with a regularly maintained blog. My thinking is, you don't have to reinvent the wheel here!

So, if you've already written blog articles, then you already have the content for your eNewsletter. At this point, just summarize a handful of your most recent blog posts, organize them into a well designed email, and distribute it to your list on a scheduled basis.

Chapter 13

Reputation Equals Revenue

In speaking at conferences to entrepreneurs all across the country about inbound marketing, I've heard the same story over and over again. Business owners and managers are feeling weighed down by not having control over their online reputation.

Perhaps you're one of the many who are being held hostage by a ripoffreport.com complaint listed alongside your website in Google's search results. Or, maybe you feel like Yelp is the mafia of the online world because they only seem to publish your 5-star reviews if you're also a paying advertiser.

Is this ethical? Is it right? Is it fair?

Frankly, the answer doesn't matter. Like it or not, it's the world we live in and it's best to be proactive instead of reactive about it. So, take a look at these 5 interesting data points along with the explanation of how they can directly influence the revenue you generate as a company.

Data Point 1: 81% of people research a company before doing business with them [GE Capital].

What This Means: It doesn't truly matter how your prospects hear about your company because they're going to research you online before parting with their hard-earned cash. It's vital to note that this is what makes inbound marketing the most important strategy to grow your business. Why? With 4 out of 5 prospects coming to you as a result of your direct mail piece, TV commercial, print advertisement, or whatever, they're going to rely on the content you publish (thanks to inbound marketing) before making a buying decision.

Data Point 2: 88% of people trust online reviews as much as personal recommendations [BrightLocal].

What This Means: It's amazing to me that nearly 9 out of 10 people will trust a complete stranger as much as a friend or family member! That being said, it is in your best interest to regularly cultivate positive reviews from happy customers.

Data Point 3: 51% of millennials say consumer opinions found on a company's website has a greater impact on purchase decisions than recommendations from family and friends [Bazaarvoice].

What This Means: Again, family and friends are set by the wayside here. Regardless, the point is that your website is an ideal place to publish the feedback you receive from customers. One way you can do this is by placing testimonials adjacent to calls-to-action (buttons and opt-in forms). Or, simply place customer feedback on every page of your website in the sidebar or header.

Data Point 4: Rubbermaid found that, when they added reviews to their free-standing inserts in newspapers, conversions for the coupons increased by 10% [Rubbermaid].

What This Means: Utilize the feedback you receive from your inbound marketing efforts in other marketing methods. Doing so will likely increase response rates.

Data Point 5: Visitors who read reviews are 68% more likely to make a purchase [Bazaarvoice].

What This Means: Be at the forefront of getting feedback from your customers through as many channels as you're able. Instead of shunning online conversations about your business, actively encourage them and your sales will likely increase as well.

3 Things: What Not To Do

Okay, so hopefully I've convinced you to take a more active role in managing your online reputation. To help you along the way, here are three strategies you should avoid:

Publish phony feedback

In October of 2009, it became illegal to publish paid endorsements without disclosure. Basically, the FTC banned the practice of paying for phony reviews and feedback and posting them online or using them in advertising materials. My thinking is that if it's against the law, it's probably not a good idea!

Have a "review station" in your place of business

I've seen businesses have an in-house computer or iPad dedicated just to customers providing feedback. This is not a good idea for a couple of reasons. First, the websites that they're leaving their feedback on may notice that all the reviews are coming from the same location and penalize you as a result. Second, a review station puts the customer in a predicament where they might not feel they can provide you with real, honest feedback.

Ignore your online reputation

It's like death and taxes. Whether you manage your online reputation or not, you can't avoid having one. So, leaving it to run wild in the hands of the public without managing it on a consistent basis is a dangerous proposition.

3 Things: What To Do

Respond to negative feedback

It may sound like a contradiction, but negative online reviews do not have to be a negative for your online reputation. In fact, responding publicly to negative feedback allows you to demonstrate your responsiveness and authenticity as a company. This is basically a way of turning lemons into lemonade because prospects will come to appreciate your transparency and trust you more.

Capture your own testimonials

I highly suggest that you don't rely solely on third-party review sites like the Better Business Bureau, Yelp, Google, and Angie's List. Be proactive in obtaining your own feedback and then utilize it in your marketing and on your website.

Encourage honest feedback

Although many feedback websites reject the

practice of "bribing" your customers to leave good reviews, it's still best to encourage them. Depending on your niche, it may be as simple as just asking every buyer at the point of purchase. Other companies may benefit from the process we utilize below.

How Our Customers Manage Their Reputation

To give you a better idea of how you might go about managing your reputation, I'm going to share with you how we help our customers do it. We call it the Reviews Multiplier System and it looks like this:

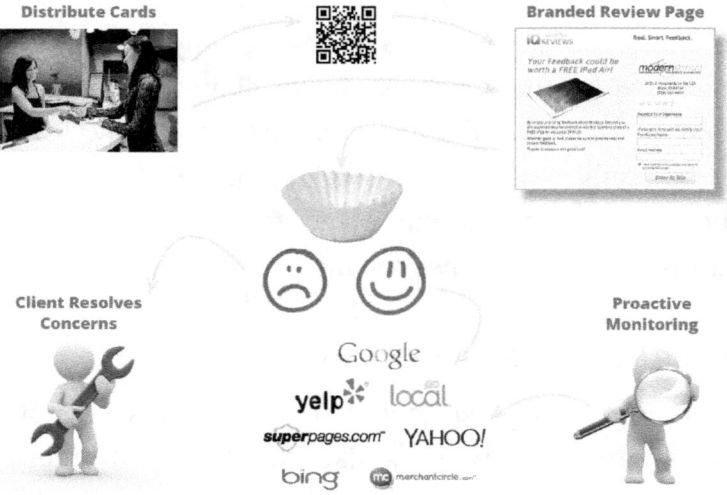

1. First, our customer hands a "review us" card to their buyer. For convenience, we design, print, and supply these cards to our customer as part of the package.

REPUTATION EQUALS REVENUE

2. From there, the buyer visits the company's custom review capture page that we created and host on one of our own review websites.

3. The buyer is enticed to leave real, honest feedback in return for an entry into our drawing for a free gift. At the time of this writing, we're offering a free Apple iPad Air. (We provide the free gift at our own expense, not our customer's.)

4. After the buyer leaves the feedback, our system filters it based on quality and rating. So, if they leave a positive review, our system will automatically ask them to also visit our customer's profiles on third-party sites like Yelp or Google. Negative reviewers don't get this invitation. Instead, they get a polite thank-you and their feedback is provided to our customer so the situation can hopefully be mitigated before it goes public.

5. The positive reviews are available to our customer to utilize in their marketing and on their website.

6. Throughout this process, we are proactively monitoring our customer's reputation online.

Now that you've seen the process our customers use, how can you apply this to your own reputation management?

Whether you utilize our system or not, be sure to

keep a close eye on your reputation. Manage it like you would any other process in your organization. Doing so will not only help you to ensure a positive online reputation, but it will positively effect your revenue as well!

Chapter 14

Finally Making Social Media Successful

All previous albums released by the superstar entertainer Beyoncé were done in traditional fashion: interviews on television, a single released on the radio, consumer brand promotions, and the like.

Her last album was different. She had none of that whatsoever.

Even so, it still sold more than a third of a million copies on the first day, surpassing the sales of her previous album in the process.

How did she do it?

She simply posted the word "Surprise!" on her Instagram profile along with the entire album for sale on iTunes. True, she was able to do so because she had 8 million followers on Instagram. At the same time, she bucked industry trends and generated a whopping $5.84 million dollars of revenue in one day, all because she had a loyal following on a single social media platform.

This ground breaking decision by Beyoncé is an extreme example, I get it. But at the same time, I get that on a smaller level social media is a powerful marketing tool that needs to be reckoned with... even if I don't personally use it.

Not A Social Media User?

Don't you think it's ironic that I'm not personally active on social media even though I own a company that regularly publishes thousands and thousands of social media posts for our customers?

Maybe you're like me where you don't get the point of social media. Perhaps you're more inclined to speak with people over the phone or in person.

Dan S. Kennedy is the world's foremost expert on direct response marketing. (Remember the Direct Marketing Triangle from chapter 5?) As the author of over 40 books, he is as old-school of an entrepreneur as you could imagine.

To that point, if you want to hire him for consulting these days, your communication must arrive in the form of a fax. No kidding.

However, Dan still uses inbound marketing tools like social media to communicate his message with his audience. I highly doubt you'll ever find Dan personally making a post on Facebook or sending a tweet on his smartphone (he doesn't own a cell phone or otherwise!). But, he does see the value in social media enough to use it as a tool in his marketing arsenal.

Here's the thing though... that doesn't matter one iota because if social media matters to your target audience, it should be important to you.

Social Media Platforms You MUST Use

First, some statistics:

- 1 in 7 minutes online is spent on Facebook
- 79% of U.S. Twitter users are more likely to recommend brands they follow
- 22% of online adults visit Google+ at least once a month

In addition to LinkedIn, Instagram, Pinterest and others, which of these should you be active on? You're probably expecting me to provide you with a list of social media platforms you should post to. The problem is, I can't.

The platforms you utilize will depend on your target audience. The question is, what social media platforms are *they* using? Then be active there.

Do you think Beyoncé would have had as many album sales if she had made the same post on LinkedIn, the popular business-to-business social media platform? Nope.

As I write this book, Facebook is a safe bet for just about every business to be active on. Remember though, we live in the digital age! By the time this goes to print, Facebook could be left by the wayside for the next latest and greatest social media platform.

The trick is to know who your audience is and be present where they are spending time online. They're consuming information on social media regardless. It might as well be yours, right?

Balance Matters

When you post to your social media profiles, try to strike a balance between being personal and professional business. Remember, it's called "social" media for a reason!

The primary goal with it shouldn't be to sell your products or services. Instead, it should build trust with your audience and every once in a while drive traffic back to your website.

A good rule of thumb is to follow the 80/20 rule. At least 80% of your posts should be social and fun instead of just talking about what you have to sell. The other 20% can be more about your company and products and services.

Scheduled Posting vs. Live Posting

Admittedly, social media can seem like a time consuming venture. To fill the need, there are some online tools and software available to help you manage and schedule your social media posts.

For example, you can create a full month's worth of social media posts, upload them one time, then schedule each to be posted throughout the following month.

Here's the thing though... Platforms like Facebook can tell whether you use software to schedule posts or if you login and do it live. They prefer live posts and in return will actually reward you by showing your post to more people. Simply put, live posting equals more visibility.

5 Social Media Best Practices

#1: Brand Your Profiles

The first step after establishing your profiles on social media platforms is to customize them with your brand and contact information.

Utilize the same colors and photos as your current website. Doing so will portray a consistent brand and image for your company online. This will also result in a perceived level of professionalism and leave a positive impression on your visitors' minds.

#2: Post Regularly

In speaking with all sizes of businesses, we have found this to be one of the most difficult aspects of social media. If you don't post on a regular basis, your at risk of making a poor impression on prospects who are researching your company before opening their wallet. On the other hand, when they see you've been posting on a daily basis, this presents your company as one that is up-to-date and has it together.

#3: Be Engaging

Imagine walking into a party and only talking to others about yourself and what you do for a living. Chances are, you're going to be looked upon as a egotistical party-pooper, right?

Well, the same goes for social media. Like I mentioned before, it's not a platform to post topics just about yourself and what you sell. So, be engaging and discuss topics that are interesting to your audience.

Keep in mind it is more difficult to connect with a business on a personal level than it is with an individual. To overcome this obstacle, consider asking for responses from your audience. Doing so will make your business more engaging.

#4: Engage With Your Audience

This tip is similar to #3, but different enough to deserve it's own section. Here, you want to actually respond to your followers when they like, comment, or share your post. A simple "thank-you" will often do the job.

Again, social media should be a two-way conversation. By responding to your audience, you're showing that you appreciate their engagement and that you're not only interested in your agenda.

#5: Outreach

By outreach I mean expanding your influence beyond just your own social media page. This is another tough one for businesses. First, it takes time to do outreach on social media. And second, there's a special approach that's necessary to take so that it's effective.

Once you've outlined who your target audience is, search for them on various platforms. See what they're posting and then determine if you should follow or connect with them. If so, periodically respond to their posts in a logical and "non-stalking" manner.

Chapter 15

Secrets to Winning Your Online Election

In a typical election, the candidate with the most votes wins, right? (Just don't ask this question to Al Gore about the 2000 Presidential Election though!)

Well, that is what off-site optimization is all about... getting more votes than your competition. Only in this case, instead of votes I'm talking about mentions, links, and citations from other businesses and websites.

To put it simply, when someone else is talking about your business online, this is essentially a vote of confidence that offers you two possible benefits:

1. Search engines like Google see these "votes." If these votes originate from a trustworthy source, they can result in more visibility on the search

engine and new traffic to your website.

2. You can obtain what is called "referral traffic" to your business, meaning the websites that mention you refer their visitors to your site through links and phone calls. Referral traffic is vital if you don't like having all your eggs in one basket with Google. This diversification of traffic is a very important benefit to consider!

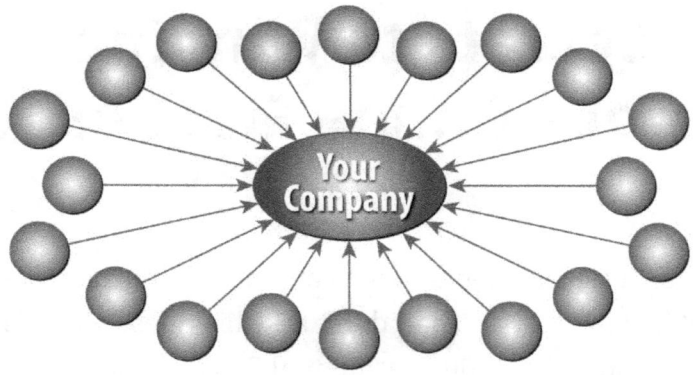

Unlike votes in an election, online votes are not counted equally. Did you notice that in the first benefit above I used the term *trustworthy source*? Let me give you an example of what I mean.

Let's say you are a pediatric dentist. From which of the following two organizations do you think it would be better to acquire a vote?

- American Academy of Pediatric Dentistry
- Billy Bob's Pest Control based in Bugville City

The AAPD of course! Here are two reasons why:

1. Search engines would be able to make a logical connection between the content (text and images) on your pediatric dental website and the content on AAPD's website.
2. The AAPD site is an authority that is well established and trusted by search engines. Who knows about Billy Bob's website, right?

Yes, the more votes you have, the better. However, I would argue that quality matters even more. Your goal should be to accumulate as many high quality votes as possible. As you do, your online visibility and inbound traffic will improve.

For The Local Business

In the second paragraph of this chapter I used the word *citations*. If you're a local business, this word is for you!

When other websites and local directories "cite" your location's contact details, Google sees these mentions as votes for that particular location.

Here are some suggestions on how to build a large pool of citations for your business:

Get Listed

If you've been in business for a year or longer, chances are you're already listed in a handful of local directories. If you're not, then the first step would be to submit a request to the site to include your business and make sure it is approved and published.

There are literally hundreds of local websites on which your business should be listed besides the major portals like Google and Bing. Here's a partial list which can change at a moment's notice:

411 Directory Assistance	CitySquares
411info	Comcast
Acxiom	Contextuads.com
Address.com	Contractors.com
Advertise.com	CrunchBase
Allpages.com	DDC
Angie's List	DexKnows
AOL Yellow Pages	DirectoryCentral.com
anywho.com	DirectoryM.com
Apple Maps	Discover Our Town
Areaconnect	Dun and Bradstreet
AroundMe.com	Elocal
Ask	ezlocal.com
AT&T	EZToUse.com
B2B Yellowpages	Facebook
BestOfTheWebLocal	fixya.com
Bing	Fizzlocal
Biznik	Foursquare
BizJournals.com	getfave.com
Brownbook	gofave.com
BuxBack	GoLocal247.com
ChaCha Search	Google
Cities2Night.com	HelloMetro.com
CityMaps.com	Herald.com
CitySearch	HotFrog
CitySlick	Indeed.com

Infignos
InfoUSA Express Update
Intelius
InsiderPages.com
Judy's Book
JustClickLocal
JustDial
Kudzu
Lexis Nexis
LikeMe
LinkedIn
Local.com
LocalMatters.com
LocalSearch.com
LookSmart.com
Loqal.com
Magic Yellow
Manta
MapQuest
MerchantCircle
Metrobot
mojopages.com
My Huckleberry
MyWebYellow
Navteq GPS
Neustar Localeze
One Call Now
Openlist.com
patch.com
pennysaverusa.com
PowerProfiles
Search Initiatives
SearchBug.com
SeccionAmarilla
seekitlocal.com
shooger.com
Siri Inc.
Snapfinger.com
SuperPages
Switchboard.com
TeleAtlas
TheRedBook.org
Topix
Tribune Interactive
TripAdvisor
Trumpet Technologies
Twibs
Twitter
Tworkz.com
USCity.net
usdirectory.com
USYellowPages
VideoPages
VoteForTheBest.com
WalkScore.com
Weblocal.ca
whatser.com
WhitePages
WhoWhere
Yahoo
yellowassistance.com
YellowBook.com
YellowBot
YellowOne
yellowpagecity.com
YellowUSA
Yelp
yipit.com
YP.com
Zipcodez.com

If this list is overwhelming to you, don't fret. Instead, create a method to systematically claim your local listings over time.

Maybe your receptionist is assigned to update one listing per day first thing each morning. (Or, you can always have us at Inbound Systems do it at a more cost effective investment.) However you accomplish this task, the benefits of more online visibility will be well worth the investment.

5 Basic Off-Site Optimization Tactics

If you choose to build these online votes for yourself, here are some ideas that may be helpful to get you started:

#1: Low Hanging Fruit

Chances are, you're already involved with some sort of organization. This could be a trade association, the Better Business Bureau, or even a charity you're involved with. If so, find out if they offer an online directory that you can get listed on and submit the request.

#2: Link Baiting

Create and post awesome content on your site. It acts as bait for other websites to link to. A blog is a great tool to use for posting interesting articles, infographics, top-ten lists, research results, and so on. If the content is engaging enough, it will attract links and traffic from other sites.

#3: Blog Comments

True, this is one of the more old-school ways of getting others to mention your website. However, it can still work! The strategy is to visit relevant blogs that are frequented by your target audience. This relevancy is important. Then, take an active part in the conversations at the end of the main articles. Many times these comment areas allow for links or contact information to be included. Just don't be too self-promotional.

#4: Approved Vendor Lists

Organizations such as universities and government agencies will often host pages on their websites listing the companies they do business with. Ask yourself, are you already doing business with an organization that does this? If not, which ones might you be able to start a relationship with? Then, get listed on their site and make sure your contact information is complete and up to date.

#5: Contributing Articles

You're an expert in your field, right? Well, there are likely online publications that are constantly looking for new and engaging content for their websites. Consider writing an interesting article and submitting it to them to be published. If you're a roofing company, I'm not only referring to getting published on roofing related websites. Anything that has to do with home improvement would be ideal.

What NOT To Do

Whatever you do, be sure to not buy links. There are companies out there that will sell you a specified number of links for a seemingly low price. However, this is a practice that is prohibited by search engines and often a tactic of low-budget, dishonest SEO companies. Buying links might work in the short term, but being penalized by Google for doing so is not worth it in the long run.

Just ask J.C. Penney. In February of 2011 the retail giant was investigated and exposed by a journalist at the New York Times for being involved in purchasing links. Up until that point they were dominating the search results and getting a lot of traffic. Then, Google looked into it the situation and promptly slapped J.C. Penney with a penalty. The company claimed to know nothing, they blamed the SEO firm they were working with, and immediately fired them.

The lesson here is that it's safer to follow the rules and only work with a third-party company you feel will do honest work. Otherwise, you run the risk of being heavily penalized by the search engines.

AFTERWORD

Congratulations! By reaching this point in my book you've shown that you are committed to growing your business with inbound marketing. Thank you for allowing me the opportunity to share my thoughts and ideas.

This might be the end of the book, but it's really just the beginning of a more profitable future for you and your company! Hopefully, it's also the start of an ongoing professional relationship where I'll be helping you get there even quicker.

The question you're probably wondering now is how to obtain the assistance of me and my team of inbounders? The next logical step is to visit the website below and take advantage of the special offer I have for you there. At the very least, you'll be able to discover more inbound marketing tips and tricks.

www.brodietyler.com/inboundbook

www.ingramcontent.com/pod-product-compliance
Lightning Source LLC
Chambersburg PA
CBHW051810170526
45167CB00005B/1953